ABOUT VERVE POETRY FESTIVAL

Verve isn't your typical literary festival. Still only four years old, it has already made a huge mark on the national poetry scene, noted for its:

Roof-shaking spoken word sets
Readings and workshops by award-winning poets
Boundary-pushing poetry/theatre performances
Lively children's events
and much, much more!

Most importantly, Verve is a festival for everyone to enjoy poetry together - where performance poets and page poets mingle and appreciate each others' art, where experimental poets swap numbers with childrens poets. Verve is for beginners and seasoned poetry afficiandos and everything in between. What ever kind of poet or poetry fan you are, no-one gets left out at Verve!

http://vervepoetryfestival.com
enquiries@vervepoetryfestival.com

Like Flyering For The Revolution

The Verve Anthology of Protest

BIRMINGHAM

PUBLISHED BY VERVE POETRY PRESS
https://vervepoetrypress.com
mail@vervepoetrypress.com

FIRST PUBLISHED FEB 2023

Printed and bound in the UK
by Imprint Digital, Exeter

ISBN: 978-1-913917-27-2

CONTENTS

INTRODUCTION by Kim Moore

I was worried when I suggested the theme of Protest to VERVE. There is nothing quite so dangerous as an idea, and once I'd let it loose in the world, I started to panic about the poems I might end up reading. Would they be too simplistic, have too many designs on the reader, would they be poems too full of anger, poems too full of complaining, too on the nose, too political, too this, too that.

There were some of those kinds of poems – but there were also so many poems full of heat and light that it felt sometimes as if they might burst into flame and burn everything around them. There were poems of anger, but also poems full of love, full of vulnerability, poems rooted in the body, poems that drew together the social, political and the personal and made those connections feel inevitable, feel timeless. I realised that voice, that part of me that was worried, was itself a product of patriarchy, a product of misogyny, a product of capitalism. That I needed to stop listening to a voice that told me what poetry should be.

Protest is one of those words that slips its own boundaries, elides its own definitions. As a noun, a protest can be a statement or action, often used as a synonym for a march against something. As a verb, when we protest, we are objecting to something. How does this play out in poetry? Isn't all poetry a protest against silence? Whenever I write something grand like that, I think of the exceptions. Some poetry is a protest against language, against the tricks and the slipperiness, the deceit of words. But maybe that is also a protest against silence.
Thank you to every single person who sent a poem to me. I learnt so much about the world from them that I didn't know before. I learnt about dictators and democracy and satire. I

learnt the name of Pinar Gultekin, and now I know I will not forget it. I learnt about the generational damage of the Spanish Inquisition. I learnt about the street dogs of Chile, who fight alongside protestors. I learnt about countries where trans people are rendered invisible, and still somehow keep speaking and living. I learnt about able bodied actors playing disabled characters and a future world where truck drivers stop and let the weeds grow around them.

To write a poem of protest is also to write a poem of hope, because if we didn't have hope, we wouldn't protest. Last night I went to a reading and listened as a male poet read a poem about his encounter with another poet who taught him about pronouns, who changed his relationship to language, and in doing so, changed his thinking. This is the possibility of poetry – not its job, or its purpose, but one possibility in a hundred, in a thousand – that a poem could change your way of thinking, maybe change your life.

I hope you enjoy reading this anthology – and keep writing, and keep protesting.

ABOUT THE WINNERS:

1ST PLACE: OVATION
In this deeply subversive poem, the poet wields satire as a weapon, exposing the fault lines and lies of dictators and the regimes they build around themselves. This poem seemed rich in references as well – I heard echoes of John Donne in here in the repeated 'Oh my dictator, my dictator' which made me think of 'O my America, my newfound land' and of course Tina Turner later on: 'Rivers and oceans are deep, but not as deep as the love of a tyrant.' I think it is a wonderful and original poem in its own right, but to send an ode that apparently lavishes praise on a tyrannical leader into a competition asking for 'Protest' poetry was a wonderfully bold and irreverent move.

2ND PLACE: IN THE PINES
This is a very different poem – it's rooted firmly in the lyric tradition and is beautifully poised. Written In the voice of Pinar Gultekin, who was brutally murdered in 2020 in Turkey, this is a haunting, haunted poem about the way a body can protest, even after death. It is a beautiful and moving piece of imagined testimony. Throughout the poem, the forest bears witness to the crime and it is tree shadows who draw 'a map in the dust' so that Pinar Gultekin can be found, and her killers brought to justice. This poem is almost unbearable in its sadness and anger – I don't think I'll ever forget it.

3RD PLACE: WHEN THEY ASK FOR PROOF
A poem that manages to span hundreds of years to examine the trauma caused by the Spanish Inquisition, and how that has played out and continues to play out through generations seems like an impossible task, but somehow this poet has pulled it off. We lurch back and forwards in time, from modern-day beurocracy to the terror of fleeing your home and your country, from the acceptable forms of proof contained in forms and language, to proof that is felt but cannot be held in your hand.

Kim Moore
The VERVE 2023 Competition Judge

Like Flyering For The Revolution

If Queer Love is a Radical Act

Becky Balfourth

Then the first hand I held was a protest,
the kind with candles and vegan snacks.

My first kiss was a placard thrust skywards,
painted with demands

Later, the nights between strangers' sheets
were like flyering for the revolution.

Relationships were throaty calls to action.
My blood was a riot of longings.

With you, I found shelter, a moment to strike my match.
Now my words are a manifesto laid on a bed of ash:

I love you. We build again from scratch.

Clause 28, Protest Snapshot, circa 1992

Fiona L Bennett

your pelvis wrapped around my thigh,
my hip cupped by your belly, our
breasts resting like eggs.
Our kiss
obliterates the policeman
standing behind us arms folded.

Take a pen and draw
around our embrace
the line creates infinity,
draws the eye more
than the placard above us--

G-E-T Y-O-U-R L-A-W-S O-F-F O-U-R C-U-N-T-S

What stands out to me now
is the pleasure on our lips,
the ugliness of the words,
how the power of change
makes its claim
over and over.

They've heard about the bees

Ros Woolner

Earth-Walker, they call me here,
the last First-Gen Settler. Lonely titles,
immortalised in a hundred homework
essays every year. The children ask me
about candles, kettles, bouncy balls.
They don't fool me. They're after
tales of burns, scalds and falling,
of airborne disease and a life behind
masks. Always the same. Tell us again.
Today I'm on strike. I imitate woodpigeons
cooing on the chimney, draw endless
variations of seashells, describe the restfulness
of green, picnics on riverbanks, woodsmoke,
plum jam, the persistence of wasps –
                                        Like bees, I tell them,

but without the honey.

Ovation

Wendelin Law

I touch myself when I see the statue of our great Supreme Leader, the colourful portrait of our Absolute Ruler, and The Little Red Book we hold high as our brightest Sun, when the East is Red. The One Man rises, stiffer than the hammer and sickle, erect with almighty powers, oh, the strongest viagra. He indoctrinates me, reeducates me, loves me more than my mother and father do. His greatness is omnipresent. His presence is unbound. He is in your classroom when you are doing math. He is in your computer when you are browsing the internet. He is in your bedroom when you are having sex. He is the court that rules by justice, who *knows* by telepathy if you are the bad egg, the spy or the traitor colluding with evil foreign powers. He is your brain cell which stops you from thinking about fr**dom--a dangerous, subversive, secessionist thought. He leads us to liberation by incarcerating us all. He is our only saviour. All hail! All hail! Our most democratic Dictator, *wàn suì, wàn suì, wàn wàn suì!* May he live more than million million years! We sing in hysteria as we are applauding together, kneeling together, being tortured (with love) into voluntary forced confessions together, until, we are run over (with love) by tanks together. Fellow patriots, compatriots and comrades, come, come, cum, cum!, the people who refuse to be slaves! In our equal paradise, there are no slaves when we all are! The masses stand up to be the owners! Let hundreds of flowers bloom in "*meí yǒu, meí yǒu, tōng guò!*", "*meí yǒu, meí yǒu, tōng guò!*" Oh, my dictator, my dictator, how you fill me with happiness, fill me with pride, fill me with ecstasy! As I put my hands together, worshipping; my clapping palms, touching and separating, touching and splitting, my soul, in constant ovation, is lusting after your every last jism of wisdom. Heaven and Earth are big, but not as big as the Party's kindness. Rivers and Oceans are deep, but not as deep as the love of a tyrant.

Step on us! Rejoice when trampled by the Party's giant footsteps.
Under our Mr. Chairman, the revolutionary country is a sea of red!

[Note: (1) "Wàn suì, wàn suì, wàn wàn suì!" (萬歲，萬歲，萬萬歲 !) is a salutation to the emperor in ancient China, which wishes him a life of million, million years.
(2) "Meí yǒu, meí yǒu, tōng guò!" (沒有，沒有，通過 !) is referring to "no objections, no objections, pass!", a Mandarin phrase that appears regularly during the voting process of China's Communist Party Congress, which begins and ends with synchronised ovations. This poem also contains references to the Chinese Communist Party's propaganda songs "The East is Red" and "Father and Mother are dear, but Chairman Mao is dearer", and slogans like "Let 100 flowers bloom" etc.]

Devi

Sujana Crawford

There are Gods in every corner.
The only thing keeping us from evicting
them is our belief that everything is still possible.

At the bazaar, incessant entreats
thrum under my feet. An eager hawker
tells me how she stayed up all night

threading serpents of *sayapatri* to help me
appease Gods lurking in every corner.
I do not haggle, ask for generous fistsful

of avir and kesari. Last week I spun my own
cotton wicks, today I choose the most ornate
of *puja thalis*. On my way home, I hand out

invitations to every God at every corner.
As the day falls, I wash, drape myself in a
jari laced sari. I dance to the rhythm

of my own hymns, take my time drawing aipan,
trace a solid boundary around myself. A new feeling
comes over me, one I lack a name for.

The Gods arrive at dusk. Mill around
and make small talk. I wait
until they undig their heels and perform my *aarati.*

Later, the *gallis* are asleep. A snore espaces a window,
a moan through another. I am led to the crossroads,
where I hold court on what is and what is not possible.

My abortion was funny (yes I cried but I don't want to talk about that part)

Gemma Barnett

I don't want to talk about the days I was made to sit with it in me.
How whiskey didn't sit comfortably anymore.
How raw kids made me feel on the street.
I'd avoid their gaze like I had a shoplifted toothpaste from boots in
my bag.

Bragged about my tits looking great hating I'd lost control of my body.

How silently I cried on a bus and not just because the screams
of a newborn sliced through torn skin
but because next to me, the women grinned at the young mum

one shared *we've been there*

and I felt like i had a secret so deep it would eat me
from the inside, spit me out so I couldn't hide.
You made your bed, lie in it.

How i worked out the birthday now it won't go away.
How I'd hoped that he would stay to lay next to me at least.

I want to talk about how I shouted

I'm having twins

to make the sin as dramatic as possible.

Friends that bought me products from lush,
said I should get knocked up more their new shampoo was to die for.

How i got my nails done bright orange before
so I'd be sure to look down at my hands lovingly,
knowing they had touched good.

How we curled up on the sofa
watched films as I cramped, kicked, took codeine generously

shall we just get high make a day of it?

Jokes about black veils, holding a funeral.
Sat laughing in the dark all afternoon.
I couldn't bare sunlight in the room.
Time wouldn't stand still even if i willed it to just for a few hours.

How we said bye-bye bitchez as I bled.
How they fed me dinner, listened

it was the day after my period I don't know how...

stopped me

don't do that, we don't care, when, if, how
shame is not welcome here now at the table

I don't want to talk about
how my phone suddenly only shows baby scans on instagram

How I didn't have the energy for an uber driver
as he spoke about the pounds knocked off his journeys.
Nausea really does hit at 5 weeks.
How I fucking hate this fucking country,
with it's new non-elected MPs
who turn up on reality tv
like they haven't go a job already.

How when I was in recovery
reality tv decided to debate what I'd done,
self congratulate the opportunity to have these
important conversations.
Love may be blind but with that lot you'd need them
to shut the fuck up too.

This country let me choose my life by post.

I want to talk about how 2 days after I'd done it
I walked home
legs stiff and slow
as though there was death in them
and I looked up at the moon
and I know moons are overused in poems
but I did
I looked up at the moon
and it was full
and the edges sort of melted, spread
as If I'd dipped it in tea
and it really took my breath away
(and not just because i was going up a steep hill)
and I said

hello moon
I choose to be up at this time with you
and not because someone needs me to
be up at this time with you
but because I
alone
choose to be here

Common Phrase

Jack Emsden

I scrub my country clean listen
to the dust newly gather
round the investment banks
of my country lick the rust
from inside the eye of my country
turn my body over like debt
in this country of door handles
helicopters public enquiries
there is embarrassment
of conviction there is fear
of exposure like a cruise ship launching
my country is an advert
simulating love I am a minor actor
in the candid opening shot
of my country or I am adjusting
the microphone on the collar of my country
ask me what my country means to me
I am a small incision in the soil
of my country I think I love my country
which is why I want to open
the shores crumble the walls
empty the accounts of my country
my country never earned it
my country is entitled as a headline
I am a common phrase in the body
of my country storming the editor's office
what is the meaning of my country
and where is it being kept let me in
help me rip it out watch it expire
like a whole forest
remembering to breathe

Parade

Nicholas McGaughey

It was the quiet I remember,
with only the sun and a few
sweepers out on the street.
I strode under the banners
past the hot dog stands,
along the empty sidewalks
towards the building,
took my place at the window,
had a sandwich and coffee
and thumbed through a book
before the bands struck up
and the streets filled
and a century stopped
in my hand.

In the Pines

Miranda Lynn Barnes

> *Five days after Pinar Gultekin was reported missing, her body was found...in a forested area in Turkey's southwestern province of Mugla.*
>
> *- Al-Monitor, 21 July 2020*

My voice comes from somewhere inside the forest.
At first tinny and strained, contained, seeping through
a rusted hole inside the oil barrel where I sleep. A tremble
in the earth rises to break the crust of concrete, unnatural

blanket. The smoke is already gone. You'd be forgiven
for thinking I was a bonfire, forest fire, a dry day's diesel,
an unwise refuse conflagration. That day was hot.
Summer bleached the green of pines, fogged the air

with heaviness. For days after, no one came. Parts of me
remembered my body, but just barely. Only the branches
above me remembered time. Summer nights in the forest
are quiet; occasional rustles echo the flickering of stars.

At first, I stayed silent, not knowing how to speak
without my lips, my lungs, my breath. Death stole
from me the chance to call for justice. But then a hum
began to rise in me—I learned it from the fungus in the dirt.

The sun rose high that morning, drew a map of treeshadows
in the dust. Footsteps arriving and gold, gold in the boughs
as light told them where to find the missing sister, daughter.
The footsteps caused my hum to waver, so I grew louder, louder.

Come, find me tangled up in roots and leaves, a pile of cinders.
Come, find me broken, come find me folded, crushed, discarded.
Come, find out the price of my refusal, the cost of saying no
to men who'd rather burn the world to ash than go without.

Fragile

Arji Manuelpillai

Tonight a home is a bouquet of cold chrysanthemums.
Tonight a man is no longer a bit chilly.

The underpass feels so spacious
funny how relief and grief sound so like brothers

sorry to bother everyone I'm homeless
looking for a place to sleep tonight.

Do you remember how our eyes dragged
the way bare feet drag on gritted roads

I gave him a tenner, I knew I shouldn't,
the lady said he'd spend it on crack

but I felt clean for a whole week
and cleanliness is closest to Godliness

and the devil was in his fingernails, his eyes
disappearing into the buttons of my coat.

Shame, it can curl like space in the underpass.
If I squint my eyes hard enough

he was nothing like me, a goblin,
an animal, death's favourite fascinator.

If you squeeze the veins tight enough
he's blue as winter. Sometimes

you wake up and you feel
like the whole city is dying,

one empty home at a time, or maybe it's just me,
dying I mean.

when they ask for proof

Casey Jarrin

(A 2014 Spanish Law opened Spanish citizenship to descendants of those expelled during the Inquisition, six centuries ago)

I dig through drawers   at the public records office
marriage certificates crumbling   flaking skin falling
births and paternity   hard to track
unrecorded blood   premature death

I can't hear their voices   no archive of first screams
atonement is a funny thing   what's that she said?
what's done cannot be undone   no do-over or second chances
a country squirms *lo siento*   I grasp for Ladino* straws

El Ministerio de Justicia   a fee to file
small bureaucratic mercies   *without renouncing citizenship or requiring residency*
but how can I know   twenty generations removed
we lose track   where are the blood-stained linens
we don't collect vials   we hoard stories

proof: *birth or marriage certificate*
in the Castilian tradition
they married young and far from home

proof: *report from the appropriate entity*
testifying to family names
Sephardic lineage
Spanish origin
they changed names wherever they went

proof: *certification from rabbinical authority*
or La Federación
they lost their trust in gods

proof: insiders and yeasayers
attorneys in pinstripes
lies rubber stamped
tightly wrapped
official fictions
watermarks
tradition

Each night I dream
in blue and clay.

*__Ladino__ (also Judeo-Spanish, Judesmo, Sephardi): after the 1492 Edict of Expulsion andmigrations from Spain and Portugal, Ladino spread across the Ottoman Empire and Europe;still spoken by Sephardic communities in the Balkans, North Africa, Greece, Turkey, Israel

Shaoshan

Christopher Horton

We went there because it was where Mao was born.
The son of a disciplinarian, forced into an unhappy marriage
at thirteen, I only later read he tried to run away.
Was he happy growing up? I asked at the time.
Of course, you said, but something made you speak quietly,
each word was swallowed back inside your throat.

The picture I took shows you looking immaculately dressed.
Your one brown suit was always unmarked. I came to learn
it matched every season and amounted to a week's wages.
The look on your face is familiar but still hard to read.
It conceals that other you, the non-tour guide version.
We only ever had the one discussion about Tiananmen.

When you finally told me about your younger brother,
it was two months on from this hot day in Shaoshan.
Difficult to comprehend the fear that would make a man
jump from the open window of a provincial lecture room
when they came for him with batons in the reckoning.
This was not the place to have that discussion,
not in Mao's own village where ladies danced and sang
to The Glorious Revolution, whilst twirling red ribbons,
and where, as my questions fell, you lost your voice.

Veins

Stephen Lightbown

Needle is here. Needle is here for you. The fourth time today,
or is it night? It's hard to tell, without windows, visitors, sleep.
You've sunken into somewhere. Needle asks is it always like this.
Yes, I say. *Make a fist*. I try not to use it. *Sharp scratch*.
Oh, fuck off needle. Needle bleeds from one person to the other.
A soft voice, an impatient voice, an exhausted, underpaid trainee voice.
Needle will pray for me, Needle asks why I use a wheelchair,
Needle asks why I use a wheelchair; Needle asks why I use a wheelchair.
It's in my notes, I don't say.

Purple bruises pool my arm where Needle searched for you.
Faces on lampposts. Drink more, drain me. I used to run
away when I was small. To be lost. Alone. To disappear.

I pull the crisp white sheet over my head, it does not smell
like home. This isn't the first head this sheet has been pulled over.
I close my eyes. Wonder what time the bats will come.

El Vaquita

Steve Pottinger

El Vaquita is one of several famous street dogs in Chile who join demonstrations, and side with the protestors against the police. El Vaquita never allowed himself to be adopted, so when he was injured by a pellet from a police shotgun and refused to be captured, no-one could take him to a vet. Knowing this, local people organised a fake demonstration on Jan 2nd 2020, which the dog then joined. The demo made its way to a vets, where El Vaquita was treated. He still joins protests in Antofagasta, and was voted 'character of the year' in the local paper.

I've always been my own master.
Howl at the moon if the fancy takes me, yes,
– who wouldn't? – but mostly all I ask
is a full belly, sunshine,
a stroll round the harbour
with a weather eye on the pescadores,
a nose in the arse of old friends,
then siesta in the afternoon.
Sniff at lampposts, scratch for fleas,
enjoy the quiet life. That's me.

I answer to no man.
But when the marching starts,
my ears prick, I slide like water
down alleyways, *calle*, slip
between legs, beneath patting hands
to the front line.

I have a nose for injustice,
teeth for what is wrong.
On our own, we are nothing.
Together, strong.
I've felt the boot of the oppressor
in my ribs before. Not having it.
No mas! No mas! No mas! No more.

A thousand curses on the bastard *policia* who shoots me.
May he never lick his own balls again
or scent a bitch in heat.
May his mother's spaniel piss in his jackboots,
smear his silken handkerchiefs with shit.

Xmas is a quiet doorway in the shade,
a dull throb, licking my wounds. But,
when my people march again,
I join them. We are the pack.
Whoever we are fighting for this time,
venceremos! No turning back.

Viva El Vaquita!
Viva... me?
Mother of God, may I be born again
a dog with two dicks.
This is solidarity, people
of my *barrio*, this is

you, *veterinario* with the kind eyes,
hands that are gentle. I won't run.
Do what you must. I trust you.
Heal me quickly – there is fighting to be done.

Despite common misconceptions circulated online, if you got suddenly sucked out of your space suit you won't explode. or (Coming out as gay won't kill you.)

Scarlett Ward

You will be asked whether you knew you were in space all along.
Your family will whisper "why did she go to space without a spacesuit?"

(You left the home that kept you alive.
It was the hardest unwombing you have ever fought for.)

You will wonder at how the darkness of space had a texture. It feels like absolute nothingness, which in itself is the softest material you have ever been wrapped in.

(You were the loneliest entity that ever had consciousness enough to yearn for touch.)

Your skin is airtight and so will cradle your organs against the jealous suck of the vacuum.

(You held yourself in your darkest moment when all else was black.)

You won't freeze. Your body will radiate its heat slowly. For a moment, you will be the warmest thing in thousands of light years.

(You found your own core to be a source of radiation.
You huddled around it like a fireplace.)

Your blood holds enough oxygen for around 15 seconds of consciousness. You will get a front-row seat to every celestial body's complex ballet.

(As you craned your neck upwards
you always knew that the stardust in your bones ached to be part of a constellation.)

You must exhale completely before your come out of your space suit. Otherwise, the residual air in your lungs will expand and rupture your chest cavity from the inside out. You must first expel everything. You will feel a sense of loss, but where you are going you can't take any of it with you.

(The first morning you woke in her arms
you never felt so free.)

falling backwards holding glass

Spencer Wood

that is how kissing him in public feels
spines bearing the brunt of opinion
so the fragile thing between us
might survive

our woven hands are noisy like hardcore
lobbed down a bucket rubble chute
echoing far beyond
their grasp

dad do you remember when I blocked
the beam of your laser level on site
and for a moment nothing
was straight

that long drag of a cigarette you take
before another funeral
that's how I kiss him
before coming home

we're the kebab shop elephant leg
a greasy love reeling in drunks
once a girl shouted at us *go on lads*
get stuck in and we did

we didn't stop

because dad when I kiss him
I'm an archer learning to play the harp
I'm a ghost who has found his sheet
I'm a little boy atop a brick wall
blowing bubblegum pursing lips
pinching bright pink air between
thumb and forefinger
holding it to the sky

and floating

remember the red

Perla Kantarjian

You must take revenge by continuing to live.
– Silva Kaputikyan

you comb your hair and there spritz its red, red flowers–
it is time for the becoming: you know.

you pick them up and thread them into the shawl
you will wrap her in when she comes.

when you will have soldiered well into the pledge.

when she comes you will name her Նանե
and baptize her in myrrh,

thumb rose water onto her cheeks
and make surc you say

Նանե, հոգիս,
this is վարդաջուր:

as well as درو ءام.

and when that first tooth stems you will
veil her face and pearl wheat, cinnamon, and honey

for the guests, pin her to her rightful pedestal
and anoint her choosing and rejoice

when she settles her fingers on the book.
and you will smile when they call her *yavrig*

as though it does not come
from the turkish *yavrum*

because, sometimes, you say it too.
and when they all leave

you will rock her in your arms, lullaby her
into her yet-still night you will pray

pray she, too, eventually understands
how a fruit of your sort without its seed

is but dust
for the earth

*Note: In Armenian mythology, pomegranates symbolize fertility and good fortune, and guardian against the evil eye. Նանե (Nane) was an Armenian pagan mother goddess. She was the goddess of war, wisdom, and motherhood, and the daughter of the supreme creator god Aramazd. "Agra Hadig" is a ceremony in Armenian culture commemorating the first tooth coming in of a newborn baby. The estimated number of the Armenian Genocide victims is between 1 to 1.5 million. Childbirth soon became a national, patriotic duty to ensure the survival and presence of Armenians given the losses and displacements.

Potato

Iain Whiteley

It is about a wasp in a fridge. It is about a wasp in a fridge when it is too early to have a wasp in a fridge. No one wants a wasp in a fridge this early, even someone looking for an idea. What happens is this: a peripheral character makes Aeropress® coffee and it is a regular morning—a bit warm for late October in Cumberland, but a regular morning it is. A dunnock sings from an apple tree. The coffee smells good and reminds the peripheral character of regular, unremarkable mornings and that is what the peripheral character thinks. The fridge door de-seals with a *jug*. The reader knows it is about a wasp in a fridge, but the reader cannot know if the wasp is in the fridge beforehand or if the electric light coaxes the wasp in. The peripheral character radiates a light-forming heat in the morning's dark, which is to say he wears a hat with an inbuilt torch. Why did the wasp not follow the hat-light? Perhaps it did. Just as the wasp is drawn to the fridge-bulb, the peripheral character is drawn to the buzz of the fridge. Is the fridge broken? No. It is a wasp in the fridge. The peripheral character can't be bothered with the wasp. It is too early for a wasp. It is also a bit late, inasmuch as it is late October. Then again, it is also a bit late for the blueberries and that doesn't stop them. The protagonist throws mashed potato at the painting. How far do the blueberries travel? Can a door *jug*? The wasp bathes in fridge-light. The wasp is enjoying the fridge.

don’t say […]*

Hannah Burrows

call me the flower but not
the garden. don’t say I’m […]
but know I am the carnation
buttonholed in your neighbour’s coat

with pansies like bruises blooming
underneath. let me be touched
only by lavender smoke, anointed
with violets winding around

this sickened head. see me grow wildly,
know the sum of my parts but not
the summer sun touching prickled stems
of legs, feeding the rootless body

that quests for steady ground—
know it is an inarticulate rebellion
to stay so stubbornly delicate
in the face of human weather.

when they ask you *what you are*
and only petals are allowed to pass your lips—
you don’t have to say you’re […]

but know one day you will walk barefoot
into the paradise of an uncontested self.

*The “Don’t Say Gay” bill was signed by Florida Governor Ron DeSantis on March 28th, 2022 and came into effect on July 1st, 2022. The bill ‘prohibits classroom instruction’ on sexualities and gender identities for children up to grade 3.

There but for the grace of God

Caroline Stancer

I want to sandwich these stories between beautiful things. That day when a pool of blue shone from the stained-glass window onto the 1000-year-old stone floor and we stood for five minutes wondering if we could swim in it. Your dog's heavy-breathing warmth as she slept next to you and greeted you with her faithful face every morning in those final years when you were so much alone because the chaos was like a razor wire fence. Your fucking style, visible at 100 paces even when you were crumpled and dirty, you could stop traffic you were so gorgeous. The alcohol dulled the edges, but you needed ever larger doses to be numb. Like swallowing a snake, some things keep poisoning from the inside. The old poet, who you so admired, who was one of your heroes, who you were so excited to see when you were 16, who signed your book, who invited you up to his hotel room *for some fun*. And when it was your beloved grandma's funeral, you made your collection of tissue flowers for her and they were beautiful, but when you spoke to your dad on the phone, he said *you're a piece of shit and you will never get anything right, not ever* and you threw all the flowers in the bin, and that wasn't even the worst of it with him.

And then, pouf,
like a light,
another collection
of your brain cells
went out.

And there was your step dad, who you trusted, who told you when you were 17 that he had fallen in love with you, and would you run away with him? You were just finding your feet, like a new-born fawn rising. You were something beautiful kicked sideways and left askew, a vein of pain running across your face. You loved your friends and you stopped coming round, and you stopped sending your eloquent cards and the guilt built up like a stack of books about to fall. Once you got lost, you were an easy target, and they would reach out their hands and twist it from the tree. How do you stop a sledge that's careering down the hill? You don't even bother to say stop half the time, you don't even bother to say it. One of the worst things when you died was the feeling that they had buried you under all their dirt. The hungry ghosts came to eat you. Or maybe you ate yourself, hypnotised. You believed so many of their lies. I carry the centre of your Russian dolls in my purse, the smallest one, and I polish it so it shines. It's not much, but it's all there is.

There Are No Soundscapes For Paraguay

Ruth Yates

There are no Cacaltaya Thunderstorms.
You cannot legally change your name.

There are no soundscapes for Paraguay.
There are no Echoes of the Night.

They do not recognise your gender.
There are no soundscapes for Paraguay.

No Windstorm in the Atacame Desert.
Yren and Mariana want to live their lives freely.

There are no soundscapes for Paraguay.
Protesting isn't easy for trans people.

No Nightsong in the Atlantic Forest.
There are no soundscapes for Paraguay.

As trans women, Yren and Mariana are busy
defending themselves against discrimination.

There are no soundscapes for Paraguay.
No Insect Symphony, no Squeaky Tree.

I came into the world to show who I am,
not to be told who I am.

There were no soundscapes for Paraguay.
Soy real, y mi nombre debe ser legal.

Don't tell us who we are.

Quotes in Italics are from: Amnesty International Write for Rights campaign and Yren Rotela and Mariana Sepúlveda's words
Names of soundscapes are from:
https://earth.fm/?ref=naturesoundmap

Still Life in Vantablack

Glyn Edwards

still life in Vantablack

i

trapping light on black plumage / the bird of paradise's turquoise collar appears fluorescent /there's deep sea footage of a fangtooth / swallowing bioluminescent fish like a black hole / scientists tried to photo the Pacific blackdragon under spotlights / it was only a silhouette / its contents stayed censored / the more light shone on some objects / the darker the void / Vantablack was exclusively licensed to a single artist's studio / BMW was permitted to coat a car beyond the black of the spectral range / thereafter it was withheld / withdrawn from commercial markets / reserved without exception for aerospace and defence sectors

ii

The Ethics Committee met to discuss Shell Oil's ongoing sponsorship of the London ScienceMuseum's climate exhibition

whether the gagging clause prohibited the museum from discrediting the reputation of the company.

iii

Ludovico Einaudi pauses in the middle of 'Elegy for the Arctic' / he looks up from black white keys / black Steinway on its white floating platform / the white sea off Svalbard / the camera cuts to ice falling from the Wahlenbergbreen glacier / the composition ends one chord early / fade to black

iv

after the Gulf of Mexico oil spill, activists poured molasses aroundthe plinth of the Easter Island statue of Hoa Hakananai'a in London Museum's Living and Dying display the BBC reported the event with no images of the protest, finished the article with the metonymic quotation importance of long standing corporate partners.'

v

vi

a man undresses in Tate London / lies on the floor in fetal position / hands covering his eyes with a white tissue / two people dressed in black pour charcoal and sunflower oil upon his white skin / in a photo taken from an upper gallery / the A4 letter beside them would look like the white rectangle of information bottom right of a sculpture / it is titled *Human Cost* / and it explains the ethical vacuum in culturewashing / the attendants aren't reading it / they talk into radios / check their phones / the gallery staff extend barriers to prevent the public seeing

Enobarbus, Octopus

Julie Runacres

This blows my heart.
If swift thought break it not, a swifter mean
Shall outstrike thought, but thought will do't I feel.
...I will go seek
Some ditch wherein to die.
Antony and Cleopatra Act 4 sc. 6

It takes something akin to autopsy to establish
death by broken heart. Enobarbus,
deserting Antony, blowed his heart
by thinking, but it took two watchmen,
unremarked in any larger story, to corroborate
he hadn't fainted, or lain down in that ditch to sleep -
- but rather died, weaponless, by willing. Margaret Radcliffe,
maid of honour to Elizabeth I, took the death of her twin brother
so much to heart, the autopsy found *certeyne stringes striped all over* it.
Sudden emotional stress, most commonly in postmenopausal
women, swells the left ventricle into the shape of takotsubo
— an octopus trap. Similarly, the mother octopus
lays her clutch of eggs and, bereft, begins to eat
herself, seeks out some ditch to die in.

Astronaut

Sue Spiers

In the way her eyes roll upwards
or develop a silver sheen
that makes you think
she's considering escape velocity,
becoming so still,
she slips into invisibility,
a stealth ship in a launch bay
so he doesn't notice
she's left the planet.

THE POETS

Becky Balfourth is a 36 year old writer of poetry and short stories from East London. She was one of eight poets selected for Griots Well in 2022. She has had work published in *Mslexia, Litro Online, Blaekk* and *The Colour of Madness*, as well as other publications. Her writing often centres around themes of mental health, sexuality and race. She also blogs at thesleevelessproject. Becky is studying for a PhD in Creative Writing, focused on Caribbean Literature. Outside of writing she enjoys running and reading and is currently learning Swahili. She has a writing residency at StoneMinimarket in London.

Miranda Lynn Barnes is a poet and researcher from the US, now living near Nottingham. Her debut pamphlet, *Blue Dot Aubade* (V. Press) was published in 2020. *Formulations,* co-authored with chemist and poet Stephen Paul Wren, is a chapbook of newly created poetic forms based in chemistry, published in March 2022 (Small Press/Tangent Books). Miranda taught creative writing for five years at Bath Spa University while undertaking her PhD. She now serves as Research Associate in Archiving & Preserving Open Access Books as part of the COPIM Project. Miranda is also an editor at Consilience Journal and co-editor of Poetrishy.

Gemma Barnett is an actor / poet / writer based in London. Her poem 'The Front Desk' won the Poetry for Good prize and was featured on BBC Woman's Hour. She was a winning finalist of BBC Words First in 2021 with 'i killed them when they came for my kids'. She was long-listed for the Evening Standard Short Story Competition 2022.. Her writing for stage includes 'Agatha' (Pleasance Theatre/Vault 5) and CPT commissioned 'Now you've learnt to talk, I dare you to sing' (shortlisted for Unlimited.) Her debut short film 'Bridge' was commissioned by the BBC and began as a performance poem at Theatre Deli for Pandemic in the City.

Fiona L Bennett is a writer, director and facilitator. She is founder of the award-winning project and podcast The Poetry Exchange. Her poems have been published in journals in the UK and USA including *The Rialto* and the *San Pedro River Review* and listed in competitions including the 2022 National Poetry Competition and The Bridport Prize. She has an MA (distinction) in poetry from The Poetry School / Newcastle University. She curated and directed the poetry of Adrienne

Rich for Ballet Black's, Then or Now choreographed by William Tuckett –The Barbican and touring from March.
https://www.fionabennett.co.uk

Hannah Burrows is a 21 year-old lesbian poet, editor and facilitator living in Birmingham. They graduated with a first in English and Creative Writing from the University of Birmingham in 2022. Whilst studying there, they became president of the creative writing society, headlined Grizzly Pear, and twice represented UoB on its Unislam team— placing second in 2021 and winning in 2022! They've been published by English Heritage, Young Poet's Network, *Olney Magazine* and others. They find inspiration in Buffy the Vampire Slayer, queer tenderness and the Norfolk coastline. Most importantly, though, they have a rescue dog named after John Keats.

Sujana Crawford is a multilingual poet, playwright and researcher, working in Nepali, English and Hindi. Sujana's creative work is driven by a fascination with people, places and folklore. Her work has been featured in various magazines and anthologies, and her radio and theatre pieces have been developed in collaboration with BBC Radio 4, Theatre Absolute and Warwick Arts Centre, among others. In her day job, Sujana works as a UX Researcher, working across the UK public sector helping research and design better IT services. Sujana was born in China, raised primarily in Nepal and currently lives in Warwickshire with her husband and two young children.

Glyn Edwards is a PhD researcher in ecopoetry at Bangor University. His second collection of poetry, In Orbit, will be published by Seren in March 2023. He is co-editor of *Modron*, and edits the Wild Words feature for North Wales Wildlife Trust. He is a former winner and trustee of the Terry Hetherington Award for Welsh young writers, and works as a teacher in North Wales.

Jack Emsden was shortlisted for the Wolverhampton Literature Festival competition 2021, and awarded 2nd place prize in the VERVE Poetry Festival competition 2019. Their work has appeared in *Ink, Sweat and Tears, Lucent Dreaming, Porridge*, and *SPAM*. They run and host Resonance, a monthly poetry open mic night in Deptford, South London.

Christopher Horton's poems have appeared in *Poetry London, Magma,*

Ambit and *The North*, as well as in anthologies with Broken Sleep Books and Penned in the Margins. He has won awards in the Bridport Prize and The National Poetry Competition. His pamphlet, *Perfect Timing*, was published by tall-lighthouse in 2021. He was also commended in the VERVE Festival Poetry Competition in 2022 with his poem 'Barbecuing in the Snow'.

Casey Jarrin (she/they) is a poet, artist, educator, survivor. Her work appears across Irish-UK-US journals: *Banshee, Abridged, Belfield Literary Review, Washington Square Review, Banyan Review, Buzzwords, Grand Journal.* She's received the Goldsmith, York, and Fingal Poetry Prizes and was honored to be shortlisted for the 2022 Bridport Prize. A Jewish-Catholic atheist from New York who's since lived in Dublin and Minneapolis, their poetry journey began at the Nuyorican Poets Cafe, exploring poems as speaking out-and-towards-others, poetry as empathy machine. She received her English BA(Yale)/PhD(Duke), taught literature-film-queer aesthetics at Macalester College, and now runs Live Mind Learning. She's completing her debut manuscript, *The Naked Dinner*. www.caseyjarrin.com

Perla Kantarjian is an award-winning Lebanese-Armenian writer, journalist, editor, and educator, with writings in 30+ publications, most recently *Electric Literature, Magma, The Poetry Society, AMBIT,* and *Lucent Dreaming*. Her work has been recognized by the Southbank Centre, the 2022 Sappho Prize for Woman Poets by Palette Poetry, the 2022 St. Lawrence Book Award by Black Lawrence Press, among others. Her poem "Half Woman, Half Starlight" is soon to be archived on the moon as part of the Artists on the Moon project by The Lunar Codex. She has an MA in Creative Writing from the University of East Anglia.

Wendelin Law (she/her) is a poet and writer born and raised in Hong Kong's concrete jungle. This city of monstrous high-rises taught her about freedom and protest. She was shortlisted for Magma Poetry Pamphlet Competition 2022 and was awarded 1st prize of Professor Shirley G.L Lim Poetry Writing Scholarship 2018. Her poetry and review have appeared in *Hillfire Anthology, Voice & Verse Poetry Magazine, Cha: An Asian Literary Journal, PN Review* and elsewhere. She holds MScs in Literature & Modernity and Creative Writing from the University of Edinburgh. Feel free to share protest poetry with her on twitter @ wendylawwrites!

Stephen Lightbown is a poet who writes extensively but not exclusively about life as a wheelchair user. Stephen has been widely published and is the author of two poetry collections for adults, *Only Air* and *The Last Custodian* (both from Burning Eye Books). In 2023 he will publish his first poetry book for children through Troika Books. He lives in Bristol in the UK.

Arji Manuelpillai is a poet, performer and creative facilitator based in London. His poetry has appeared in magazines including *Poetry Wales, The Rialto* and *bath magg*, and his debut pamphlet, *Mutton Rolls*, was published with Out-Spoken Press. Arji was shortlisted for the Oxford Prize, the Live Canon Prize, the National Poetry Prize and the Winchester Prize, and was runner-up in the Robert Graves Prize. He is a member of Malika's Poetry Kitchen and London Stanza, received an Arts Council England award to develop his creative practice, and worked with Hannah Lowe as part of the Jerwood/Arvon Mentoring Programme. His debut collection, *Improvised Explosive Device,* was published in 2022 by Penned in the Margins.

Nicholas McGaughey lives in the South Wales Valleys. He has poetry in *Stand/Bad Lilies/The Friday Poem/The London Magazine/Poetry Wales/Poetry Salzburg* and *The Atlanta Review* amongst others.

Steve Pottinger is a poet, author, and founding member of Wolverhampton arts collective Poets, Prattlers, and Pandemonialists. He's an engaging and accomplished performer who has performed at Ledbury and StAnza poetry festivals, at the Edinburgh Free Fringe, and in venues the length and breadth of the country, from Penzance up to Orkney. His sixth volume of poems, *thirty-one small acts of love and resistance* is published by Ignite Books.

Julie Runacres grew up in Leicestershire, and is contemplating a return after a career in teaching English, most recently in West London. She veers between being thoroughly sedentary — writing poetry, the odd short story, aspirational crochet projects — and overdoing it by distance running, weight training and on the yoga mat. Her poetry has been published in *14 Magazine* and *Long Poem Magazine*, among others. She is a member of the Crocodile Collective.project Finding the Words, developed by Anvil Arts, where he takes down the words of participants and turns them into found poetry.

Sue Spiers lives in Hampshire. Her work has appeared in *Acumen, Dreich, The North, Spelt* and on-line at *Atrium, The Wine Cellar* and *Ink, Sweat & Tears*. One of Sue's poems was commended in the Poetry Society's stanza competition in 2020. Sue's poems have been commended in Binstead, Hysteria and Ware competitions in 2022. Her work will appear in the City Space Project exhibition in Portsmouth (Feb/Mar 2023) – a collaboration between photographer Janey Devine and Tongues & Grooves poets. Sue supports the Winchester Poetry Festival and the spoken word group Winchester Muse. Sue tweets @ spiropoetry.

Nottingham poet **Caroline Stancer** has been a counsellor and trainer for many years. She completed the pamphlet *This Weighted World* on the MA in Creative Writing at Nottingham Trent University. She won the Stonewood Prize for Regional writing (2017), was longlisted for the Primers competition (2019), longlisted for the National Poetry Competition (2022), and has had poems published in the journal *Otherwise Engaged*. She produced the pamphlet *Full Body Rclaim*, working with Helen Mort on the Writing East Midlands Mentoring Scheme. Caroline is currently writing the second draft of a novel. She is the co-founder of Nottingham poetry collective Dandelions.

Scarlett Ward is a Queer Staffordshire Poet living with Multiple Sclerosis. She was shortlisted for the Women Poets' Prize and the Spellt Poetry Competition in 2022. She was selected for the room 204 cohort by Writing West Midlands and she came in the top 10% of the Bridgeport poetry Prize. Her recent work was published in Nine Arches' *Under The Radar Magazine, 14 Poems* and Broken Sleep.

Iain Whiteley has spent twenty years writing for advertising agencies, design agencies and museums. You can find his poems in *The North*, at The Poetry Archive and on *The Friday Poem*. A collection *Ping!* is published with Write Bloody UK.

Spencer Wood (he/him) is a writer and teacher living in Leeds. His poetry can be found in publications such as *Fourteen Poems, Alchemy Spoon, Modern Queer Poets* and *Untitled Writing*, alongside upcoming work in Acid Bath's *Pocket Anthology of Addiction and Recovery* and the ekphrastic focused journal *After*. Spencer recently graduated with an MA in Creative Writing from the University of Leeds and can be found running a monthly LGBTQ+ Drama Club for Leeds Community Consortium.

Ros Woolner lives in Wolverhampton and is a member of Cannon Poets and Bilston Writers. She won the Guernsey International Poetry Competition in 2021 and was shortlisted for the Women Poets' Prize (run by the Rebecca Swift Foundation) in 2022. Her debut pamphlet, *On the Wing*, is available from Offa's Press, who will be publishing a new collection of her poems in summer 2023.

Ruth Yates lives in Sheffield. Her poems have been published in online projects e.g. the Writing Squad's Staying Home, and in magazines and anthologies including *Introduction X: The Poetry Business Book of New Poets, The North, Route 57* and *Pennine Platform.* She was awarded a Sheffield Writer Development Grant in 2022.

ABOUT VERVE POETRY PRESS

Verve Poetry Press is a quite new and already award-winning press that focused initially on meeting a local need in Birmingham - a need for the vibrant poetry scene here in Brum to find a way to present itself to the poetry world via publication. Co-founded by Stuart Bartholomew and Amerah Saleh, it now publishes poets from all corners of the UK - poets that speak to the city's varied and energetic qualities and will contribute to its many poetic stories.

Added to this is a colourful pamphlet series, many featuring poets who have performed at our sister festival - and a poetry show series which captures the magic of longer poetry performance pieces by festival alumni such as Polarbear, Matt Abbott and Genevieve Carver.

The press has been voted Most Innovative Publisher at the Saboteur Awards, and has won the Publisher's Award for Poetry Pamphlets at the Michael Marks Awards.

Like the festival, we strive to think about poetry in inclusive ways and embrace the multiplicity of approaches towards this glorious art.

www.vervepoetrypress.com

@VervePoetryPres

mail@vervepoetrypress.com